MISSOULA-BITTERROOT MEMORY BOOK
A Picture Post Card History

D1609115

GREETINGS FROM Missoula

THERE WAS SOME THING DOING EVERY MINUTE at the Great Ravalli County Fair, Hamilton, Mont.

MISSOULA
— BITTERROOT —

N'B HIGGENS AVE, LOOKING NO. MISSOULA MONT,

MEMORY BOOK

A
PICTURE POSTCARD
HISTORY

By Stan Cohen and Frank Houde

Library of Congress No. 79-90794
ISBN 0-933126-09-3

First Printing November, 1979

Cover Art Work By Monte Dolack

PICTORIAL HISTORIES PUBLISHING COMPANY
713 South 3rd West • Missoula, Montana 59801

TABLE OF CONTENTS

Introduction..i
Picture Post Card History ii
Bridges...1
Business and Industry...3
Churches..16
Flood...18
Fort Missoula...22
Government 25
Hospitals..28
Houses..30
Organizations 33
Parades and Fairs 34
Railroads 38
Schools...44
Street Scenes 48
University of Montana...57
Miscellaneous 61
Darby..71
Hamilton..72
Stevensville 78
Victor..82
Bitterroot Miscellaneous..83

INTRODUCTION

Picture post cards produced from 1901 through the 1940s can tell us much about the history of Missoula, the Bitterroot Valley, and the surrounding valleys. This was a period of rapid growth, when the area changed from a raw frontier to becoming the modern center of Western Montana. By 1950, Missoula was a trade, government, and education center, and the Bitterroot Valley had become one of the region's major agricultural areas.

Many of these cards were originally printed in Germany. Some are in color, and the earlier cards are of superior quality. However, the color cards of the 1930s and 1940s are of much poorer quality. Since many of these cards are in color, but are here produced in black and white, some detail has been lost.

Not much is left of the houses, buildings and other sites depicted here. It might be well to reflect on what is left, and work to preserve our remaining historical sites.

The cards are all from the collections of Stan Cohen, Frank Houde, and Ford Knight of Missoula, and represent selections of the best cards produced on the area in the past half-century. Many, many people helped with the facts about the different sites. They are too numerous to mention, but it was very enjoyable working with the people in the community on this project. We hope this book will give the people of the area a better insight into its early Twentieth Century history.

Stan Cohen
Frank Houde

A BRIEF HISTORY OF PICTURE POSTCARDS

Picture postcards are like a window into the past. They enable us to see not only what the towns around us looked like at the turn of the century, but also how the people in those towns dressed, worked, and played. Postcards of that era cost only a penny to mail, and were used in much the same way we use the telephone today. They were sent to relatives and friends to mark everything from birthdays to trips to political gathering.

Postcards are the best record we have of the early photographer's art. The excellent quality of the photographs and lithograph printing methods used to print most of the old postcards will never be seen again. These have been lost to the speed and efficiency of modern technology.

One of the most interesting changes the postcards show is in the area of transportation. Watch how postcards with street scenes show the emergence of the auto as our main mode of transportation. Early scenes show no automobiles; street scenes from 1908 to 1920 show both horse-drawn vehicles and autos. After 1920, horse-drawn vehicles were seldom seen.

The first picture postcards were printed in Europe about 1863 and were intended to provide an inexpensive way for people to mail a short message. In May of 1893 the U. S. government issued the first U. S. postcards. They commemorated the Columbian Exposition in Chicago, Illinois. The private sector could not print postcards until May 19, 1898, and then only with the words "private mailing card" printed on the back of each card. On December 24, 1901, one last government regulation came. It ordered the word "private" deleted, leaving only the word "postcard" on the back of the cards.

After the change in government regulations in 1898, many U. S. publishers jumped on the postcard bandwagon. Many of the cards in this book were printed by companies which made outstanding views of nearly every city in the United States. Two of the largest and most famous of these companies were the Detroit Publishing Company, and the Edward Mitchell Company, of San Francisco. Their cards are exceptional because they show busy street scenes and people going about their everyday life.

Many of the cards were published locally. Two of the best known of the local publishers were the Charles E. Morris Company and the McKay Photo Company. Morris opened a photography shop in Great Falls, Montana, in 1910, after ten years' experience around the Chinook area. Most of his cards were printed in Germany because the Germans used superior printing methods at that time. Morris lived in Great Falls until his death in 1938.

R. H. McKay came to Missoula from Oregon in 1905. He owned the McKay Art Company until his death in 1960. Most McKay cards are real photos, and seem to have been printed in his own shop.

We owe our thanks to these men, and ones like them, for providing us with a photographic record of this era.

The Higgins Avenue Bridge looking south. The first bridge was built in 1873 by John Rankin.

The Higgins Avenue Bridge in 1919. This was built after the 1908 flood washed out the previous bridge. The present bridge was built in 1963.

The Parkway (Orange Street) Bridge in 1946. It was built in 1937.

The Blackfoot River Bridge at Milltown. This bridge was built in the early 1900s and torn down in 1949 to make way for the present bridge built in 1950.

Mapes and Mapes Shoe Shop in 1910. It was located at 214 South
Higgins and is now the location of Barry's Shoes.

The Minute Lunch in the 1920s. Located at 222 North Higgins, the
building is now the site of the Kiddie Shop.

The second Florence Hotel Building at the present site. The first building was built in 1888 by A. B. Hammond and named for his wife. The building burned in 1913.

The Florence Hotel fire on September 24, 1936.

The Florence Hotel Building in the early 1940s. The building was built in 1937 and operated for many years as Missoula's largest hotel. It is now called the Glacier Building.

LOBBY—HOTEL FLORENCE, MISSOULA, MONTANA

Lobby of the Florence Hotel in the 1940s. Rates were $2.00 up.

The Independent
Telephone Building at
207 East Main Street, in
1912. It later housed the
Missoula Chamber of
Commerce and now the
District II Human
Resources Council. It
was built in 1905.

Independent Telephone Bldg, Missoula, Montana. 200?

The Palace Hotel
Building in the early
1900s. It was built about
1906 and was originally
known as the Savoy.

The Kennedy Hotel at Circle Square in the early 1900s. It is now the Park Hotel building.

The Harnois Theater in 1912. It opened in 1908 on East Main Street next to the old Chamber of Commerce Building. It was torn down in the 1960s. It was one of Missoula's most popular theaters.

The Hammond Block at the corner of Higgins and Front was built before 1900 and burned down in 1932. The present building was built in 1934.

The First National Bank Building in 1909. The building was built in 1891 and demolished in 1962 to make way for the present bank building. It is the oldest bank in Montana, established in 1873.

12525. Montana Block, Missoula, Mont.

The Montana Block Building in 1917. The building was built in 1910 and houses the Western Montana National Bank (now the First Bank — Western Montana).

Scandinavian American Bank Building at the corner of Broadway and Higgins. The building was torn down in 1956, and the Western Federal Savings and Loan Building was built in its place. The savings and loan company was started in 1911.

Scandinavian American Bank Building, Missoula, Mont.

The Higgins Block on the corner of Main and Higgins. It was built in 1889 by C. P. Higgins, and is the oldest major building in downtown Missoula. It now houses the First Federal Savings and Loan, shops, and offices.

The Penwell Block in 1912 at the corner of Higgins and 3rd. It now houses businesses and apartments.

1128. Smead-Simmons Building,
Missoula, Mont.

The Smead-Simmons Building on Higgins Avenue was built in 1921. It now is the Wilma Building, housing the Wilma Theater, shops, offices and apartments. At one time it had a swimming pool in its basement level.

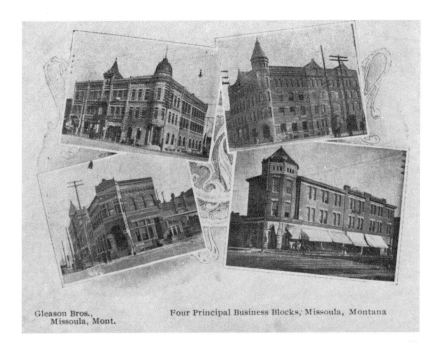

Gleason Bros.,
Missoula, Mont.

Four Principal Business Blocks, Missoula, Montana

Four principal business blocks in Missoula in the early 1900s.

United Clothes Shop at 314 North Higgins is now occupied by
Wyckman's Office Supply.

G. T. Meade's store on West Broadway is now the site of the
Greyhound Bus Station.

RETAIL STORE OF MISSOULA MERCANTILE CO.
MISSOULA, MONTANA.

The Missoula Mercantile Building in 1912. The company had its beginning in 1877 as the Eddy, Hammond and Company. The first building constructed at that site was built in 1877. The present building ws built in 1904. It incorporated the 1877 building.

The Union Market on Front Street. John R. Daily is second from left. It is now the site of Wide World of Travel.

The Star Garage on Main Street in the late 1930s. It is now a restaurant and disco club.

Mix and Sons Market at 204 South 3rd Street West is now occupied by the Bitterroot Music Store.

Big Blackfoot Milling Company at Bonner in 1907. It was started in the 1890s and later became the Anaconda Copper Company's main sawmill. It is now a large lumber operation owned by Champion International.

Birds eye view of Bonner in the early 1900s. A railroad bridge is being built in the lower left.

The First Methodist Episcopal Church on Main Street was built in 1911, with the east addition constructed in 1963. The congregation was organized in 1871.

The Presbyterian Church at 235 South 5th Street West. It was built in 1916. The congregation was organized in 1876.

Interior of the Catholic Church, Missoula, Montana.

Interior of St. Francis Church. The paintings were done by Brother J. Carignano over a period of approximately ten years. They were finished in 1908.

St. Francis Xavier Church and Catholic Schools in 1923. The church was built in 1892 and is still in use.

No9 CATHOLIC CHURCH & CATHOLIC SCHOOLS MISSOULA MONT,

The Higgins Avenue Bridge was washed away on June 5, 1908, during the great flood.

A temporary walkway for foot traffic was constructed a short time after the washout. A new bridge was constructed in 1908-09.

Two views of Missoula during the 1908 flood. Looking to the South Side.

The Blackfoot River Bridge in Milltown, at flood stage. The Anaconda Company Sawmill is in the background. Logs are piled up on the bridge.

The Bitterroot Trestle washed out during the 1908 flood.

The Orr residence is seen floating down a creek (possibly the Rattlesnake) during the 1908 flood.

Rattlesnake Creek overflowing by the Greenough Mansion during the 1908 flood.

Views of Fort Missoula in the early 1900s. The only building still remaining is the Post Exchange Library and Gym.

Fort Missoula was on the outskirts of Missoula from the time it was established in 1877 to the 1920s or '30s.

The old barracks at the Fort are now used by the Army Reserve and the U. S. Forest Service. They were built in 1908-11, with alterations in the 1930s.

The drill grounds and officers' houses at the Fort. The houses are still in use, housing local military personnel.

Barracks of '78, Fort Missoula, Mont.

One of the original barracks at the Fort, built in 1878 and later used as an officers' club. It burned down in 1973.

Headquarters, Fort Missoula, Mont.

The headquarters building at Fort Missoula in 1917.

View of the Missoula County Courthouse about 1915. It was opened in July of 1910. It was designed by A. J. Gibson.

Missoula County Court House,
Missoula, Mont.

The Missoula County Courthouse in 1916. The new wing was added in 1966. Eight historic murals painted by Edgar Paxson are located in the building.

The Federal Building and Post Office was built in 1913 and now houses the downtown post office branch (Hellgate Station) and various government offices.

FEDERAL BUILDING, MISSOULA, MONT.

The Federal Building and Post Office in 1936. The east addition was added in 1928. The Forest Service Building to the north was built in 1936.

The Public Library Building on Pattee Street was built in 1903 at a cost of $12,500, using Carnegie Foundation money. It now houses the Missoula Museum of the Arts.

In 1912 a second floor was added to the library, at a cost of $9,000. The present library building was opened in 1974.

An early view of St. Patrick Hospital building, built in 1889. The hospital had been established in Missoula in 1873 by the Sisters of Providence.

The newer part of St. Patrick Hospital was built in 1923, and the original building was torn down in 1964. The newest addition was built in 1952.

The second building of the Northern Pacific Beneficial Hospital was built in 1892. The hospital was established in 1884 for railroad employees.

The present building of the Northern Pacific Hospital was built in 1917. It is pictured here in 1918. It is now the Missoula General Hospital.

Houses on Gerald Avenue. Both of these houses are now fraternity houses at the University.

More homes on Gerald Avenue. The middle house is the Peterson Mansion near Hellgate High School. The other two have been torn down.

The Greenough Mansion estate in the Rattlesnake area. It was built in 1894 by Thomas Greenough, a well known area businessman. It was moved to the Farviews area in 1965 to make way for Interstate 90 and is now a restaurant and golf shop.

The residence of E. L. Bonner, a prominent area businessman, was built in 1893 on Gerald Avenue, across from Hellgate High School. It was later called the Spotswood Mansion, and was torn down in 1959.

Residences in Missoula in 1910.

A good buy in 1907.

The Masonic Temple, at the corner of Broadway and Pattee, before 1920. The building was built in 1909 to house the various Masonic orders. The Masons were organized in Missoula in 1868. The building is still used as a Masonic Temple, along with various businesses and offices.

The Elks Club Building at Pattee and Front Streets during World War I. It was built in 1911, and the first floor was used by the Missoula Mercantile. Hellgate Lodge #383 was established in 1897.

Plate exhibit at the Western Montana Apple Show in Missoula in 1910.

First premium (McIntosh apple) at the Western Montana Apple Show, 1910.

Indians on parade in downtown Missoula in 1917. Probably part of the Missoula Stampede Celebration.

Indians on horseback in front of the horse stable at the Missoula County Fairgrounds. The stable was built in 1912 and has since been torn down.

Soldiers from Fort Missoula parading down Higgins Avenue near Broadway on July 4, 1910. In August of that year these troops were called out to help fight the great forest fires in Idaho and Montana.

Cowboys at the 1916 Missoula Stampede. In 1915, C. M. Russell and Edgar Paxson, two well known Montana artists, rode in the Stampede parade.

Parade in downtown Missoula (Higgins Avenue). Probably one of the Missoula Stampede parades in 1915, '16 or '17.

Another view of an early parade in Missoula.

A post card view of Missoula and the Northern Pacific Roundhouse in 1883. The railroad came through Missoula in that year, the same year the town was incorporated.

Bonner's first street cars. These were owned by the Missoula Street Railway Company and were built in 1910. The last street cars ran in 1932.

1133 — NORTHERN PACIFIC DEPOT, MISSOULA, MONTANA.

The Northern Pacific (now Burlington Northern) Station was built in 1901 and is still in use.

The Northern Pacific Station in the early 1900s.

N. P. STATION AND CAR SHOPS, HELL GATE CANYON IN BACKGROUND,
THE GATEWAY TO MISSOULA, MONT.

Northern Pacific Station and car shops in 1910. The present roundhouse was built in 1924 and 1936 and partially torn down in the 1960s.

NORTH COAST LIMITED LEAVING MISSOULA, MONT.

Steam engines at the Northern Pacific Station in 1913.

The Chicago, Milwaukee, St. Paul and Pacific Railroad Station
was built in 1910. It is still standing.

Mount Jumbo and steam engines along the Clark Fork River.

Marent Threstle, 226 ft. High, Missoula, Mont.

The Marent Trestle just below Evaro Hill is 226 feet high and was built in 1883. At the time of its construction, it was the highest wood railroad trestle in the world. It was replaced by steel in 1885.

Fish Creek Trestle, 146 Feet High, on the Coeur D'Alene Branch of the N. P. Ry., near Missoula, Mont.

The Fish Creek Trestle west of Missoula on the Coeur d'Alene branch of the Northern Pacific Railway. It was built in 1914 and is 146 feet high.

The Bitterroot Special of the Northern Pacific Railroad takes a header on January 9, 1911.

A wreck along the Clark Fork River in the 1940s.

Missoula schools in 1909. Central School was built in 1887, and housed the first public high school classes in Missoula. The South Side School was constructed on the present Willard School site. It also housed high school classes, and, later, the University of Montana, until 1899.

Missoula schools in the early 1900s.

New High School, Missoula, Mont.

The first building occupied by the Missoula County Free High School, on South 6th Street West. It was built in 1904 and was the high school from 1906 to 1908. It then became the Roosevelt Grade School, and is now the School District One Administration Building.

10351. Garden City Business College, Missoula, Mont.

Weber & Avery, Missoula, Mont.

The Garden City Business College at 120 North 4th Street West. It was founded in 1893 and is now called Babs Apartments.

The Missoula County Free High School was built in 1908, and designed by A. J. Gibson. It was remodeled in 1913 and gutted by fire in 1931. It is now part of Hellgate High School.

Hellgate High School on Higgins Avenue in the late 1930s. It incorporated the 1908 high school building, with many additions through the years. The north wing was built in 1921 and the south wing in 1931. Sentinel High School was opened in 1956.

Sacred Heart Academy on West Pine Street in 1909. The original
building was built in 1885 and added on to in 1900. It was a Catholic
girls' and co-ed school until the late 1970s, and was demolished in
1979.

Music rooms of Sacred Heart Academy.

North Higgins Avenue in 1907.

Higgins Avenue looking south in 1913. The *Missoulian* occupies
the tent site now.

Higgins Avenue and Lucy's Furniture Store, around 1918. The
furniture store building was built in 1909.

Higgins Avenue looking north in 1913. The Daly Addition street
car is in the foreground.

Higgins Avenue looking south in 1917. The Missoula Bank of
Montana Building occupies the Donohue site now.

South end of North Higgins in 1918.

Higgins Avenue in 1927.

Night scene on North Higgins Avenue in the early 1900s.

The best lighted street in America, Higgins Avenue.

Higgins Avenue at night in 1911.

Higgins Avenue in the winter of 1913. The Belmont Hotel building
to the right is still standing.

Corner of Higgins and Broadway in 1911.

Higgins Avenue in the 1940s.

Front Street in 1910.

Front Street looking east in 1910.

East Front Street in 1907.

East Main Street in 1908. The *Daily Missoulian* Building to the right now houses the Dutch Boy Paint Store.

Cedar (Broadway) Street showing the two bank buildings.

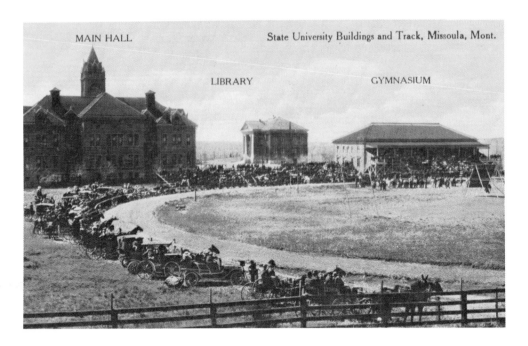

University buildings and track in 1908.

View of the University during the 1930s.

Main Hall before 1920. Constructed in 1898, it is the oldest
building on campus. It now serves as the University
Administration Building.

Science Hall was the second building constructed on campus in
1898. It is now called the Venture Center.

Craig Hall was constructed in 1902, and was originally the first women's dormitory. It has been renovated, and is now the Math Building. It was named for Oscar Craig, first President of the University.

The old library building was constructed in 1908 and now houses the Psychology Department. It also housed the Law School for many years.

The football field in the 1930s. The original track was constructed in 1902, and the football field in the 1920s. The field was moved to its present site in 1968 to make room for the new Mansfield Library and University Center.

Gymnasium, State University, Missoula, Mont.

The first gymnasium, constructed in 1901, was demolished in the early 1960s. It was located just north of Main Hall.

Aerial view of Missoula in the 1940s. The city had spread out on both sides of the river and into several side valleys by this time.

View of Missoula in the late 1930s. The south side still had a lot of vacant areas.

The original Higgins and Worden store at Hellgate Village west of Missoula on Mullan Road. It was built in 1860 and torn down in 1935. Hellgate Village was the forerunner of present day Missoula.

View of Missoula in 1936.

Ex-President Theodore Roosevelt speaking from the corner of
the Western Montana Bank Building on April 11, 1911. He was
running as a candidate for President under the Progressive
Party.

The entrance to Greenough Park in 1909. The park was donated
to the city as a Christmas present on December 22, 1902 by Mrs.
Thomas Greenough.

Yandt's Mens Wear at
403 North Higgins
burning on New
Year's Day, 1942.

Boy Scouts in front of
the 1917 fire truck at the
fire station at the corner
of Ryman and Main
Streets. Probably in the
1930s.

A summers snow on Mount Jumbo on August 24, 1910. This is the snow that put out the great forest fires of 1910 in Idaho and Montana.

The school bus that ran from Fort Missoula into Missoula in 1910. Tommy Touchie was the driver.

The first load of sugar beets being unloaded in Missoula, October 8, 1917. In the past, sugar beets were a big crop in the Western Montana area.

Mount Jumbo and houses along the river in the early 1900s.

47. Reservoir, Missoula Water Works, Missoula, Montana.

The reservoir on Water Works Hill in 1908. The first wooden reservoirs were built on the hill in 1880. This reservoir was built in 1908 by the Missoula Light and Water Company, the forerunner of the Montana Power Company.

Big Blackfoot Dam, Missoula, Mont.

Simons' Art Store.

The Big Blackfoot Dam in 1906 above the sawmill.

24. Clark's Dam and Power House, Missoula River.

Clark's Dam and Power House on the Missoula (now Clark Fork) River in 1908. It was built in 1907 by the Missoula Light and Water Company.

Rattlesnake Dam, Missoula, Mont.

The Rattlesnake Dam near Missoula. It was built by the Missoula Light and Water Company.

The Blackfoot River
road near Missoula. The
first road was built
along the river in 1936.

A log jam on the
Blackfoot River in 1908.
These logs were going
to the Anaconda
Copper Company's mill
at Bonner.

Log Jam on the Blackfoot River, Missoula, Mont.

69

Bison at Moiese north of Missoula. The National Bison Range was established in 1908.

A band of Flatheads on the Reservation in 1908.

Main Street looking south around 1920.

Main Street looking north around 1920. Darby was founded in the
1880s as a lumber and trade center.

Main Street, Hamilton, Mont.

Main Street of Hamilton looking west in the early 1900s.

53922   Main Street, Hamilton, Mont.
3/20/07
Photo by J. C. Conkey.

Main Street in 1907. The big building in the center is now the Banque Restaurant.

Court House and School House, Bitter Root Valley, Hamilton, Mont.

The courthouse and school in the early 1900s. The school was
built in 1893 and was later used as the courthouse annex. It was
torn down in 1975. The courthouse was built in 1900, and is now
the Bitterroot Heritage Center.

CITY HALL AND CHAMBER OF COMMERCE, HAMILTON, MONT.

City Hall and Chamber of Commerce in Hamilton. The building
was built around 1900 and is still in use.

THE RAVALLI
HAMILTON, MONT.

The Ravalli Hotel in 1912. Marcus Daly built this large hotel in 1893, and it burned down in 1919. The Elks Club building now occupies the site.

The U. S. Public Health Lab in the 1930s. The lab was established in the Bitterroot Valley in 1910. The present building was built in 1928, with additions in 1934 and 1937.

The Service Flag Of Hamilton, Mont. Raised 3/9/18, Has 112 Stars.

Raising the service flag on Main Street in March, 1918. The second building from the left now houses the *Ravalli Republic* newspaper. Howard Parker is making a speech from the car at the right.

Saw Mill, Hamilton, Mont.

The Anaconda Copper Company sawmill, built by Marcus Daly in 1890 at the west end of Hamilton. It was torn down in the late 1930s.

The Daly Ranch house in 1908 near Hamilton. This house was built by Marcus Daly, and it burned down in 1908. Daly's ranch encompassed over 22,000 acres in the Bitterroot Valley.

Daly's second residence was built by Mrs. Daly in 1910, and has not been used for more than forty years.

One of the lanes on the majestic Daly Ranch near Hamilton in
1909.

Birdseye view of Hamilton from the roof of the Ravalli Hotel in
1908.

Main Street in 1909.

Views of Stevensville in 1916.

104—Ruins of Old Fort Owen, near Stevensville, Montana, a relic of the Indian Wars

Ruins of Fort Owen just west of Stevensville. It was built in 1850 by John Owen, and is Montana's oldest white settlement. It flourished as a major trading center until 1872. Part of the original building is still standing.

St. Mary's Mission in Stevensville was built by Father Ravalli in 1866. The Mission was founded in 1841 by Father DeSmet.

The Stevensville Public School in 1913. The school was moved in 1924. The building has been remodeled, and it now houses the United Methodist Church.

The old high school was built in 1901 and is now the junior high school. This view is from 1909.

Dr. Thornton's Hospital on East 3rd Street in 1912. It is now the Stevensville Rest Home.

The Baptist Church at the corner of Church and 4th Streets in 1919. It is still in use.

55—Looking East on Main Street, Victor, Montana

Main Street in Victor, looking east, in 1909. Victor was laid out as a town site in 1881 by Judge Frank Woody of Missoula, and it was incorporated in 1887. The railroad station at the end of the street was moved in 1929 when the tracks were moved to the east.

Victor School, Victor, Mont

The Victor school in the early 1900s. This building was torn down in 1963 to make way for the present building.

The Charlos Club House south of Hamilton along the Bitterroot River.

Presbyterian Church, Corvallis, Mont.

View of the present Corvallis Community Church in the early 1900s. It was built in 1884 for the Presbyterian Church which was combined with other Corvallis Churches in 1915. In 1945 the Community Church was organized.

83

Digging Irrigation Canal of Bitter Root District Irrigation Co.
A Slight interruption.

A steam engine wreck on the Irrigation Canal in 1908.

Digging Irrigation Canal of Bitter Root District Irrigation Co.

Digging the Irrigation Canal or "Big Ditch," in 1908. This ditch carries water from Lake Como north past Stevensville.

Logging in the Bitterroot Mountains in the early 1900s, before logging trucks were used.

Another horse-drawn logging scene in the early days.

Sleeping Child Hot Springs Hotel around 1920. The springs were discovered and used by both whites and indians in the 1880s. The hotel burned in the 1920s.

The bath house at Sleeping Child Hot Springs south of Hamilton. It is now a popular resort.

Picking McIntosh apples at Lake Como in the early 1900s. Apples were a large agricultural crop in the valley in the early part of the century.

Apple pickers near Darby.

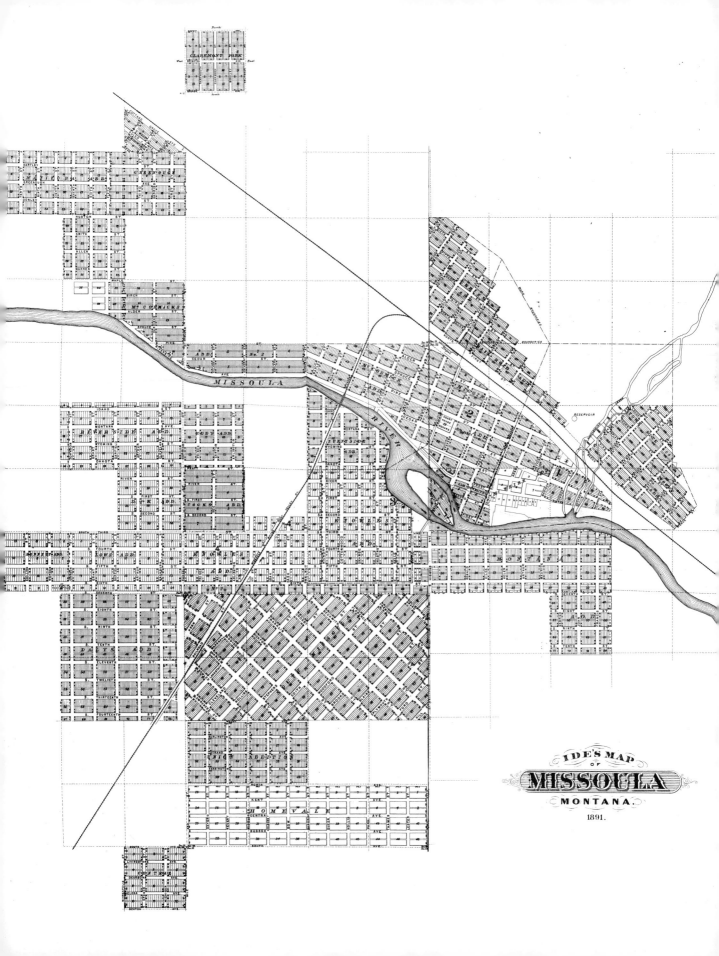

IDE'S MAP
OF
MISSOULA
MONTANA.
1891.